ART
ON
STONE

BY
THE AMERICAN INDIAN
IN
NEW JERSEY

A. R. COMUNALE, M.D.

VANTAGE PRESS New York Washington Hollywood

"The roads you travel so briskly lead out to dim antiquity, and you study the past chiefly because of its bearing on the living present and its promise of the future."

—Lieutenant General James G. Harbord

CONTENTS

ILLUSTRATIONS

PREFACE

Archeology of the American Indian of New Jersey has progressed beyond the stage of the classification of a hobby. It is no longer a novelty to merely collect and display artifacts, pottery or trinkets, because an unexplored field of Indian art work on stone is now presented for scientific study.

The varied challenging mystery surrounding the life and habits of the early American Indians of the State of New Jersey has remained in an unexplored state for too many years.

The unexpected accidental discovery of Indian art work on stone by the wife of the Author, increased the desire to pursue the further collection of similar and more complex material for scientific study. This aggressive approach was made feasible by the purchase of a tract of land on which an Indian campsite existed.

A wealth of geological and mineralogical material also became readily apparent on the land which is located in Frankford Township of Sussex County.

The compositions consisted of many simple to the complex intricate patterns, the latter included especial designs and phases not yet determined and must be studied in a scientific manner for clarification. A few anthropological notations have been recorded.

A peculiarly selective early boyhood environment resulted in the finding of the first argillite artifact, which created a hobby of long standing.

Residual evidence of the former Indian life became readily apparent, such as the trails along the course of the brook which led to such appropriate approaches for crossings in a number of places. One had to hop and skip over the various sized, age-old discolored gray boulders in order to go across to the opposite side of the stream. These boulders were conveniently placed in this manner by the Indians. It was with joy and as a feat of accomplishment to be able to ford the babbling brook without getting ones' feet wet because some stones were occasionally very slippery.

A burning unsettled question persisted. How did the Indian in the State of New Jersey really look? Where did they obtain the strange argillite specimens that these people used?

Mystery surrounded the grayish white mounds of clam shells which were intermingled with the dry decaying large oyster shells. They could be seen clearly above the tall green grass in the summer time. A large irregular stone "crushing" hammer with a groove, around which a wooden handle was apparently used, now gone forever into the soil due to decomposition, was picked up nearby.

One wondered in amazement at so many chestnut and hickory nut trees which seemed to be concentrated in certain areas, in the forest.

Fresh water springs with their crystal clear cool water were well known, the areas surrounding these water holes were a favorite "stopping place" for the Minisink Indians who came down from the north on their way to the seashore. Campsites nearby included many archeological artifacts, especially those of the argillite series and battle axes which were made of the granitic stone found mostly in the northern part of the State of New Jersey.

Exploration over the years extended to areas farther away. It was noted that certain strange colored grayish or brownish stones, which stood out boldly and were found easily on the surface of the ground, came from some distant place. These argillite specimens are very numerous in campsites of Sussex County. It seems that there is some mystery concerned with the origin of the argillite stone.

Reference is made at this time to the loss of three early collections. The hobby of collecting Indian artifacts was almost discarded with the loss of the three accumulations. One in a schoolhouse was destroyed by fire, of unknown cause. A second one was taken by theft and dispersed indiscriminately about the neighborhood by a boyhood neighbor. The third collection contained a very highly prized granitic battle axe. It measured approximately six to eight inches in length, with a smooth groove encircling the handle area. The cutting edge was sharply bevelled and unmarred by defects. The most remarkable part of the rounded head above the groove consisted of an area of ruby red Indian paint which appeared encrusted. A slight bevelling from usage is noted on the opposite side of its circumference. This individual who resided in Ridgewood, N.J., purchased it unwittingly from a member of my family without my permission. Many years later I visited her in this northern suburb and refunded the five dollars to her with the anxious expectation of recovering this stolen item, but she stated that someone bought it from her, the identity remaining unknown. Perhaps some museum now has it on display.

Historically the American Indian has been described with adverse distasteful qualities and no less a savage. The art work on stone by these aborigines is superlative. The "Tracing-Drawings" which have been accurately transcribed from many of the stone specimens, illustrate a very high degree of art culture. A method is described in which the art compositions have been transcribed according to the actual size. An attempt is also made to separate some of the factual material. Its essence may be reported when much of the recent new material shall have been compiled at a later date.

ART ON STONE
BY
THE AMERICAN INDIAN
IN
NEW JERSEY

OBJECTIVE PRELIMINARY REPORT

WITH DESCRIPTION

OF SITE AND GEOLOGY

The early American native was erroneously called Indian by Christopher Columbus on the assumption that he had reached India, the jewel of the East, by a shorter route westward across the unchartered Atlantic Ocean in 1492.

Anthropologists and others have proven scientifically that the prehistoric aborigines of the North American continent were of Asiatic origin.

In a series of land and sea migrations these nomadic, restless tribes crossed over from Asia into Alaska. They eventually spread fanwise over Canada to the east and south as well as the United States. With the passage of time the entire North American continent was inhabited with a robust bronze-colored people and later classified as the Red Man.

As with any given race of people, dialects appeared in the language as a result of the geographically isolated groupings or settlements, but the inherent deep-rooted customs, rituals and general forms of expression persisted.

It seems that an advanced center of art culture existed in the northwest corner of New Jersey. The natural beauty and serenity of this rolling alpine mountainous area of Sussex County, with its large dairy farms and estates neatly situated among nature's numerous fresh water streams, lakes and forests, is called "God's Country."

The "Minisinki" or Minisiki Indians lived in this region. Minisink island is located in the upper Delaware River. The famous "Council Fires" are located in the area.

Important chieftains and members of tribes held rituals and discussed the problems of the day. Important decisions were concluded around these "Council Fires."

The celebrated Minisink trail apparently started from this focal point, uniting with the accessory and subsidiary pathways, going in an easterly and southerly direction to the Atlantic coast, as far south as Atlantic City.

Numerous useful varieties of stone were easily available for the manufacture of weapons, tools, maps, effigies, sculpture, pictographs and multigraphs.

In 1912, the author's first argillite artifact was found on a farm in Middlesex county on his way to school. In 1940 an unclassified specimen, at the time, was later determined to be related to the art work discovered in Sussex county, which is approximately eighty miles away. This chalky white argillite specimen was a surface find from the Raritan area of Readington Township. The tract of land on which the site is located was purchased in the early fall of 1959. Many surface specimens for study were collected through 1961, and a few have been obtained several inches beneath the soil.

In Volume II, page 281, Figure 311, of George Catlin's book, he states, "Of these kinds of symbolic writings and totems recorded on [rocks] and trees in the country, a volume might be filled." Whereas Catlin alluded to this art work on stone, there is no description or painting by him.

From the evidence at hand, the American Indian, or prehistoric man, left behind as their memoirs by the use of precision workmanship on stone the culture of the people of the era, maps of places that were noteworthy, animal life and actual photographic likenesses of themselves.

A series of over one hundred and fifty illustrations were transcribed from the actual size tracing prints.

The site is situated in Sussex County in the upper northwest corner of New Jersey. Stokes State Forest and Culvers Lake lie in a northerly direction from the site about two miles away. Trails which now form winding county roads traverse the northerly route up along the elevated tortuous shoreline to emerge in a cleft in the mountain. The 206 highway is joined. To the north it follows the Delaware river and to the south to points such as Lake Hopatcong, the largest fresh water lake in New Jersey.

Much of the animal life still persists unhindered in this remarkable area. The two poisonous snakes, the copperhead and the rattlesnake, are found here under the rocks which will be described.

The geological varieties at the site include the sandstone, both the soft brown and the harder gray. The argillite series are both gray and brown, very much softer than the hard, colored granites. The sandstone is also combined with the conglomerates. The argillites were used extensively for weapons, maps, implements, ornaments and the surfaces for pictographic and multigraphic compositions. The granite specimens are very hard and heavy.

Among the varieties of trees noted in the second growth of the wooded areas are the following: oak, maple, cedar, hemlock, dark and white birch and hickory. Blighted stands of the native chestnut trees lie in a ragged fashion on the floor of the eastern border.

Old thickened grape vines are entwined skyward on the tree trunks. The younger vines grow spontaneously in the open field among the blueberry and blackberry bushes. In the springtime, sweet wild strawberries are found in abundance among the colorful profusion of the mountain flowers.

Many of the larger fieldstones, which were removed years ago with horses, are piled into long stone fence rows. Among the red, brown and purple varieties are a few milky white calcites and an occasional fluorescent franklinite. This latter has been mined commercially about ten miles away. Zinc was separated from the ore. Lime is obtained from the pure calcite deposits in Franklin, N.J.

In both the granitic and conglomerate varieties, because of their hardness, the subject matter has a "straight-line" method, whereas in the less hard sandstone or the argillite variety, a "circular" type engraving is observed.

There are combinations of varieties of stone, such as the gray granitic sandstone, flinty gray argillite and granitic quartzite. With the exception of the sandstone and argillite, when thrown or struck against each other an electrical spark is emitted. This physical phenomenon of "drawing fire" is readily apparent in the dark or evening.

Extraneous depositions or inclusions occur on some of the specimens. A large number of the sandstones have a coating of a dark inorganic, minutely granular adherent carbonaceous material, which is imbedded, and it is difficult to wash off. The clinical material is destroyed if a wire brush is used. Some of the brownish sandstone has a thin coating of grayish or reddish substance which is also difficult to remove. The clinical work appears to merge into it. The part of the stone which was removed from the soil is usually discolored by the muddy yellow sand and clay. This is easily washed off with clear water.

The argillites which were exposed to the weather have either a light gray or brownish-yellow powder coating. The

18

subject matter may be superficial or deeply engraved. This powdery substance, which is the result of oxidation, should be only lightly dusted or washed in clear water without scrubbing.

All of the sandstone which lie on the forest floor have a brownish discoloration. The stones imbedded in the leafy black silt of the stream have a brown-black or sooty color, except for the top of the stone, over which the water has rushed by. This oxidative process is a result of the interaction by organic matter, dampness and the acidity of the soil. Occasional specimens were noted here.

The assortment of implements, weapons, tools, effigies and markers, pestles and mortars, were ground surface material. With the exception of one yellow, jasper arrowhead, several granitic sandstone pestles and mortars, the collection of knives, spears, arrowheads, drills, scrapers, axes, small ornaments and scalping knives which are flaked and circular are all argillite. The effigies are predominately sandstone, numerous, vary in size from small to very large. They occur as carvings, sanded or flaked on the granitic variety.

The nature and extent of this material for study include the following: portraits, single and multiple, silhouettes, animal life, which indicate the source of food supply, maps which appear to show trails, lakes, mountains, possible division of hunting land and on one, the rulers of the divisions; also carvings and sculpture, effigies and pictograms.

A list of some of the animals depicted include the following: deer, moose, birds, nesting bird with eggs, snakes, fish, turtles, eagles, and woodchuck.

Many of the engravings are illustrated with multiple characters. By simple rotation of the stone specimen, the reversibility of character or subject is demonstrated. The

19

following change is noted on a specimen . . . head of an eagle to head of a snake to head of a deer faun.

The mechanism of workmanship is highly skilled and complex. Part of the edges or surfaces are smooth on the granitic sandstones and on some of the argillites, whereas the center has the subject matter brought into relief. There is a "straight-line" demarcation of subject in the rough granitic conglomerates. Sculpturing and flaking are noted on the hard quartzite and on the dark flinty argillite. Both the "circular" and "straight-line" engraving occur on the argillites and common sandstones. It is not known whether drills, hard quartzite points or some carborundum-like points or knives were used. Many specimens have a combination of sanding, polishing, sculpturing or flaking. Mineral depositions or inclusions are utilized for tone, color and delineation of subject matter. Quartz and silicates are usually deposited along fracture lines or strata.

The brown sandstone and the gray granites were commonly used for profiles, both single or multiple, especially on the periphery or external circumference of the stone. Usually the same precise elaborate details are noted on the harder stones, but only with a single subject.

The gross appearance of the specimens may be oval, square, elliptical, or peg-shaped. This latter type was apparently used to place into the ground as a marker. The elliptical, "carved-out" type may have been used to hold water or to cook food.

The arrangement and structure of the artistic work denotes precision. A single design is designated as monographic and with the portrayal of more than one, it is multigraphic. When the stone is rotated at different degrees there may be a change in the nature of the subject.

20

From an extensive amount of material on hand, a series of over one hundred and fifty specimens have been transcribed to date.

The method used in this procedure is as follows: the stone is carefully washed in clear cold water, without scrubbing, and allowed to dry thoroughly, then studied by observation. The outline is followed lightly with a soft black lead pencil. Tracing at this time is unsatisfactory because of possible blurring. If the background is light, black India ink is applied on this outline, or if the stone is too dark, red India ink is applied. A thin wooden applicator (physician's) beveled to 45 degrees works better than a fountain pen or ballpoint. Parchment paper #100 is placed over this outline, being held firmly in place with plastic tape to avoid slipping. Hard lead is not used because it sometimes perforates the tracing paper. Carbon copy paper is then placed over heavy white art paper. Above the carbon copy is placed the parchment paper tracing. A colored wax pencil is now used in following the lead outline, which prevents reduplication. The transcription is finally completed with India ink, using the beveled applicator.

A physical phenomenon of some stones is their ability to become translucent when wet. The degree varies with the quartz and calcite content. When dry most stones appear rather dull, but as soon as they are moistened, the underlying color appears and its brilliance diminishes when the moisture evaporates. The exposure of color is dependent on the inherent mineral and chemical composition. The depth of the color varies in proportion to the amount of the mineral constituents. The yellows, tans and browns predominate.

21

Great significance was attached to the reddish or purplish stone which occurs so abundantly in Sandyston Township. It is not comparable to the quality of the blood-red stone which is quarried by the present day Indians in Pipestone, Minnesota.

The phenomenon of fluorescence is observed in the stones found in certain parts of North Jersey, which have been quarried mainly for their zinc content during recent years.

The natural physical color characteristics of stone was apparently utilized. Advantage was taken of the combination of colors resulting from the complex basic mineral constituents. When the dull hard shell is denuded of its cortical layer, there is occasionally exposed a specific underlying color. If polished or sanded, it appears enriched.

According to the Indian legend, the origin of the blood-red quality of the stone is derived from the bodies of their ancestors. Ceremonial pipes and calumets are made from "catlinite" which is quarried in Pipestone, Minnesota. Arrangement of treaties, acquisition of land and the termination of wars were concluded over the ritual of smoking the "pipe of peace."

The first white man to see this unusual stone was George Catlin, who gave such an accurate description of the quarries that the smooth red stone is called catlinite in his honor. He lived among the Indians of the plains. In his travels from 1829 through 1838, he made numerous paintings of "important members" of the various tribes of the Indian nations. He remarked that only "important individuals had the right to be painted."

In his book, Volume II, page 281, he describes the Indians as "ingenious and have much in their modes and manners to enlist the attention of the curious. Songs are written in characters on these charts."

Several methods are used to determine the age of the stone, one of which is the chemical analysis of the amount of carbon (C-14) that is present and results from the chemical combustion of uranium content to lead.

The period of the art work, however, while speculative, may be computed indirectly. One is the comparative study of the workmanship and the nature of the degree of precision with the artifacts accompanying the collection. There appears to be a direct relationship between the numerical average of prehistoric and historical specimens in a given site. An indirect general computation may be made from the carbon studies of the "fire burns on stone."

For the sub-surface, from which specimens are either brought to the surface by the use of bulldozers, or natural hillside erosion, comparative determination of the age is made by the fossil beds which occur in the soil strata.

"The roads you travel so briskly lead out to dim antiquity and you study the past chiefly because of its bearing on the living present and its promise of the future"— Lieutenant General James G. Harbord. [125th Anniversary, 1837-1962, from page 8, "The Medicovan."]

Man's early attempt to exist, keep warm, obtain food for himself and his family, to seek the protection from his natural enemies required daring, cunning, brute strength and the knowledge of the application of any advantageous method for survival, either alone or in groups.

The Indian knew by instinct and training from his day by day experiences and close observation the "signs and tracts" made by animal life in passing over the snow, in the mud, over wet or dry leaves or along the banks of running water or on trees, as well as the significance of the cry of different birds, nearby, in the woods or overhead. The "signs and tracts" observed in their daily lives had a direct influence on their artistic mode of expression. The multigraphic compositions appear to portray some of this basic concept.

The Indian "war-whoop," which pierced the silence over the hills and valleys, has become a legend. Except perhaps for its mimicry which may be heard, like "Bugle Ann," on a cold chilly winter night by the north wind as it slashes through the leafless trees and buildings that are covered by nature's elements of the season.

Each long summer trek to the seashore was probably made also by the women and children as an instinctive, preventative health measure to correct the dietary deficiency. The tribes of the north traversed the smooth-beaten paths, perhaps in single file along the streams and easily accessible terrain of the Minisink trail. Sea food such as the salt water fish, clams and oysters are the natural sources for the vitamin derivatives of A and D and including organic iodine and the essential salt derivatives. Sources of vitamin C were obtained in the spring and summer liberally along the route, such as cranberries, beach plums, blueberries and others. It is interesting to note how far inland some of these oyster mounds have been observed, before the surge of modern housing developments.

The vitamin deficiency diseases, such as ricketts and scurvy were combated by the utilization of the fish oils which contain vitamins A and D, and the generous supply of fresh fruit and berries. Thyroid deficiencies were corrected and prevented by eating shell fish, salt water fish and the concomitant cooking of seaweed. The whole fish, clams and oysters, were placed over a slow burning wood fire, which usually was located in a depression in the sand, then the entire pile of food material was covered with moist seaweed. This method of baking over a slow fire in a sand pit was accepted by the early white settlers and the name of "clam-bake" remains.

Apparently the early Indians had good eyesight and strong bones. From the general appearance of the portraits and profiles there is displayed a fine neck line in both male and female. There seems to be no evidence from a physical viewpoint of goitre or thyroid disease.

Historians believe that the errors in spelling of the names of towns and places were attributed to the deficiency or lack of a common written Indian alphabet. Some think that pronunciation was misunderstood. One can surmise the difficulty the Indian had in understanding the speech of the English and Dutch language in translation.

However, it was a common practice for the Indian to use symbols and signs. He preferred to elaborate with maps, pictures and multigraphs to illustrate a point. The basic requirement of the time was to secure food and obtain protection from his natural enemies. The introduction of the white man to the Indian resulted in the severe unaccustomed changes in the life of the red man. It initiated a significantly new era for the aborigines on the entire North American continent. After many years of bitter struggle, we finally see the introduction of a new mode of life, education, the adaptation to become useful citizens, learn skilled trades and unless one is told that the individual was of Indian ancestry, it would be difficult to recognize him by the clothes he is wearing. A preliminary objective report was made in 1960, in which a method was described for the recovery of the complex, actual size arrangements of the art work on stone. These were called "tracing-drawings."

In 1961 a series of over thirty specimens was obtained which consisted mostly of portraits, silhouettes, profiles and multigraphs. The majority of these were on the red variety of stone.

There was a deficiency of color and for this reason the architectural framework, especially in the multigraphs, would ordinarily be hard to understand. The original plates of tracing-drawings were preserved. Exact copies were made. The application of color provided an aid in its proper perspective and visualization. Thus, an attempt is made to reproduce for further study the mechanics, artistic architectural quality and its implied purpose of expression.

There apparently existed among the tribes a select talented few who were adept in the mechanics of the stone art work reporting, embellishing ornaments, making effigies, portraits, silhouettes, crude maps on stone and markers for direction or other purposes.

Maps describe by the use of lines and symbolistic designs the trails, the nature of the land, water courses, lakes and mountains, the possible division of hunting land and/or the area governed by a specific chieftain. On each of the stone maps, an interesting detail is observed. One or more profiles are present, suggesting either the signature of the author-artist or the dominating ruler or rulers of the area so specified. My attention was directed to this subtle device by a contemporary artist, many years ago. The oil painting had no signature, but among the characters reposing gracefully on a horse was the artist himself.

The definition of a stone depends on its relation to the

viewer. A child in the country is attracted to it by its color and as a play thing. To man, the jeweler, its valuation as a precious gem. The geologist and mineralogist are interested in its mineral and chemical composition, whereas the anthropologist and related scientists consider it in relation to man and the ages.

The recognition of Indian art work on stone is not always simple or easy. Previous study and preparation are essential. The finding of artifacts indicates the area of a campsite or hunting area. The unusual smoothness on one surface may be suggestive. There is a certain degree of "pleasantness" or fit when held in the hand due, perhaps, to the sanded worn effect and usage.

Special features include significant clues such as the engraving marks produced by the circular and straight lines which appear throughout and the true circle, such as the spherical eye on the effigies or markers. The circular engraving on a portion of the face appears to follow rhythmically down the nose, mouth and chin. The straight lines in one or more planes are used as division markers for the art work. They do not usually follow the geological stratification of the stone. The division planes are especially noticeable in the multigraphs, in both the flat surface and the convex, irregular ovoid hard stones.

The depth of the architectural framework is different in the various stones. The argillite series appear to be superficial and may be covered with a patina of gray or brown, if found on the surface. This is the result of a chemical process from its mineral composition. The reddish or coppery colored stones appear to have a deeper outline, probably because the work required was more difficult.

The gross specimens in either small or large effigies

require no special effort, because they are self-evident in outline proportion and description.

Indian art on stone may be divided into the following general classification: Pictographs, portraits, silhouettes profiles, effigies, multigraphs and maps.

The basic architecture is the circle and straight line. There is a certain mechanical precision in the blending of one subject matter with another, especially noted in the profiles and silhouettes. Combinations of characters, such as animal life alone or with man are frequently observed in a subtle manner.

Symbols and signs are depicted within the basic framework, which in the author's series lack color. However it can be observed that some latitude has been reserved for the elective use of color. In following the architectural pattern, one notes the precise directional approach for the application of the brush strokes. The composition usually contains a dominant figure or subject, and one or more secondary figures, blended together in a precise mathematical manner.

The position of the subject material may be located in various angles. Its relation depends on the view taken by the observer on the plate. Profiles may be observed directly in the center or internally, about the edges, periphery or circumference on rotation, and also in a reverse position of the plate.

The type of stone utilized in New Jersey appears to be that indigenous to Sussex County, such as the dark gray argillites, reddish sandstone, the hard gray granites, the white calcites and the gray conglomerates.

The surface area may be flat and smooth or convex, ovoid and round. The average dimensional area involved in the series is approximately 3"x3" to as much as 10"x12".

28

Animal life indigenous to the area is frequently a subject for illustration and is commonly found on the argillite stone.

A slight preponderance apparently exists of the male over the female illustrations.

Pictographs are usually depicted with characters in action. Except for the mineral content of the stone for color, this series lacked the apparent application of specific hues. If any were used, time, the elements and chemical reaction erased it. Only in dry caves and arid climates can it remain preserved for so long a time.

Effigies are either carved, flaked or smoothed out by some form of sanding. They display the anatomical features and the stone used may be of various types. The common softer variety of sandstone apparently was utilized more often. The only color noticed is the natural display from the mineral composition of the stone.

The multigraph, as its name implies, elicits many interesting and diverse qualities. The basic architecture is peculiarly specific. The projections include several or multiple features. Besides the principle subject, one discovers the presence of many others. When the plate is reversed, there is revealed another separate and distinct illustration.

Rotation of the plate in either a clockwise or counterclockwise manner will usually indicate the presence of one or more profiles.

Subtle divisions are occasionally observed in one, two or more planes. In the multiple division planes, the lines appear bisected, between which is distinct subject material.

In a single division plane, the multigraph may show two or more sets of profiles, one facing to the right, the other to the left. Also a type in which one faces the right or left in an upright position, whereas the other is in an upside down view. On full rotation the positions are reversed.

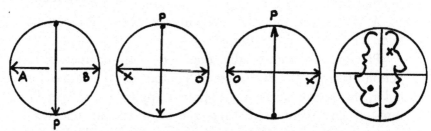

In the multiple division planes the lines appear bisected at various angles of demarcation. The lines may be straight or the mechanical architecture of the profile may be utilized, especially its periphery. The division planes which are bisected permit separate illustrations on the other side. It may possibly indicate the working mood of the artist, or that the work was completed at a later time of day or week. It may simply indicate the addition to the record.

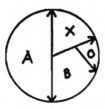

It would appear that the artist produced the art work either in stages, due to insufficient time, or incorporated separate extra material in his report.

A rhythmical artistic coalescence of structure, one with another, is observed. A large surface area appears to be reduced to a smaller one, without losing its essential identity. It is maintained by using one or more sides or surfaces of the same structural element through the use of straight and circular line forces.

The multigraph illustrates a principle by which the reduction of a given combined surface area to a fraction or percentage is accomplished without the loss of its essential structural elements or area, and it is maintained by the utilization of one or more surfaces of the same structural element, with the combination of circular and straight line forces.

The comparison of the quality, efficiency and the precision of the art work on stone may be made with the accompanying artifacts. Usually the argillite series denote an older period than the tools made of quartz, jasper and the variegated colored flints that show a higher degree of flaking. The argillites appear to be sanded and sharpened by the rubbing of two surfaces. The primitive effigies are not ordinarily flaked.

In general the works of art on stone depict the areas of the head, neck, chest, and the upper portions of the body.

Some of the anthropological features observed include a common similarity in the aquiline nose. The lips do not appear to be grossly exaggerated. The attempt to portray the anatomical features of the eyes varies in technique and description. Each artist has applied his own specific method. On the portraits and profiles the neck line, by gross appearance, does not indicate any medical evidence of goiter or thyroid disease.

The American Indian in New Jersey from the records depicted on stone appears to have been a healthy, stalwart, vigorous, proud race, and very capable of providing and maintaining the essential necessities of life for his family and the tribe.

The upper part of the body was depicted more often. It appears that this part of the torso was considered more important and descriptive than the lower extremities. The portraits, profiles, silhouettes and effigies are examples of man's desire to record for the future the accomplishments, the vanity and beauty of the person and social life of the day in that part of the country.

The circular and linear engraving marks throughout the framework appear to give direction for the elective applicator of color in the reproduction for illustration and the purpose of demonstrating the intricate details involved for proper perspective and visualization.

DESCRIPTION
OF
1960 SERIES

Three flat rectangular argillite specimens have a dominant profile in each composition. The countenances of plates 21 and 23 are more youthful than that in plate 59. The features in plate 21 are directed to the right. After shading this area, the remarkable details are brought into focus, such as the symbols for the eye, possible tribal markings on the face and the classical depiction of the contour lines of the forehead, nose, mouth, chin and neck. The illustrated details of the headdress are also noteworthy.

Both plates 23 and 59, besides the profiles being directed to the left and apparently one seemingly older than the other, are similarly arranged in a two-thirds view. Two eyes are observed, proportionately placed, so that their countenances are focused in a rather good photographic position for study.

Plate 23 measures 4 inches x 3¾ inches; plate 59 4 inches x 4¼ inches; No. 21 is a 5 inch x 3½ inch size argillite stone. Together with X-I, the possibilities for practical purposes would seem to indicate a sort of hair adornment worn by the women of the tribe, as observed in a few compositions where the hair appears tied or held up in the back.

Plate No. 0 is a large triangular argillite stone whose composition measures 9 inches x 6 inches. From the intricate maze of detail and a careful scrutiny of the contour outline, one concludes that this unusual specimen is surpris-

33

ingly an unsuspected full profile of a squaw in a sitting position. At the apex, the head, which seems to be covered or adorned, and the facial features are directed to the right. The entire body appears to be fully clothed snugly with a robe which extends upward to the back of the head with a decorative neck piece dropping downward to the neck-line where strands of material are used to tie it around the neck or collar area.

In the center and lower two-thirds of the composition, there would seem to be a suggestive silhouette or profile of a very small baby nestled in its mother's arms.

By the same token, when the facial features are studied one would determine the approximate age to be that of a young woman of child bearing age, between eighteen and twenty-five years old.

Plate 142 is a granitic sandstone specimen, size 9 inches x 4 inches, profusely and densely illustrated with numerous multigraphic signs, symbols and profiles in a cylindrical scroll-like effect. The stone borders or the periphery of the specimen has effigy counterparts of profiles which face to the right and others to the left.

The circular-straight line, complex maze is skillfully and uniquely blended with each descriptive, subtle, symbolistic design.

Plate 58 is also an intriguing multigraphic composition on a gray granitic sandstone, size 6 inches x 3 inches at the top, and with a base of 4 inches. The general profile is directed to the right and would appear to indicate, by the swinging arm-forearm and hand motion such as walking. The head and trunk seem to bend forward, and across the back is observed something being carried, which extends above the shoulders in a knapsack effect.

On closer scrutiny numerous profiles which are directed

to the right form the physical qualities of the neck, chest and stomach areas. One or more profiles which face the left compose the structural elements of the knapsack over the back and shoulders.

Plate 116, 3"x1½" is a composition of the portion of the head of a copperhead snake. This reptile was well-known to the Indian. The lethal bite produced by the teeth and poison in the sac was greatly feared. The toxic material is emitted from this poison sac in the mouth and deposited in the perforating wound produced by the teeth during the bite.

The illustration shows in detail the scaly covering of the skin, the pointed head and the mouth with the small eye, just above the division of the mouth and nose. In life it is found usually under rocks and other unsuspected places, coiled up and well hidden. It is known to blend and disguise itself with the surrounding copper-colored foliage. When it is disturbed it slithers away very quietly through the grass, after which one has difficulty in discovering it again.

Counterclockwise rotation reveals a profile directed to the left. The hair braids appear coiled or tied, which forms the right border. Clockwise rotation depicts a silhouette with the facial features, neck and chest facing the right. The former hair braid is now substituted for feathers in the upright position and the headdress is well-designed.

Plate 112 A-B-C, size 3¼ inches x 2½ inches on an argillite stone, is a typical multiphasic pictographic composition. The reversibility of character is demonstrated by three distinct species of animal life. Most prominently displayed is the head of a rattlesnake which occupies the left horizontal two-thirds portion. The nose and mouth is coiled to the right. The neck and part of the body extends to the right. The piercing eye which is observed in the central area of the head is favorably situated, because it also substitutes for the eye of an eagle in the same horizontal plane. The beak of the bird is noted to the extreme left below the rounded top of the plumed head. The larger headfeathers follow the contour and border of the entire right side. From the lower portion of the beak is located the mouth and smooth downy feathers of the neck which extend to the lower right border. This view may be visualized more clearly when the snake's right nose, mouth and right border of the neck is not so heavily outlined, and contrariwise when the extreme right border with the horizontally placed feathers are brought into closer relief in the foreground.

Clockwise rotation reveals a baby deer faun with the head and facial features directed to the right. The common eye now appears a bit slanted downward. And the rear of the head, which was the beak of the bird, is now replaced by the semblance of a faun's ear, and the nose and mouth of the snake is activated into a narrow snout of the deer faun. The neck and upper portion is common to both deer and snake.

The rattlesnake is still found in many undeveloped, rocky, mountain areas of Sussex county. Occasionally they wander close to gardens and barns. When the natives discover them they are promptly destroyed. Whereas a rattlesnake is said to give a warning signal by the vibrations of the bones which compose the tail-end piece, unsuspecting individuals may not always hear it and if carelessly stepped on, the snake will strike and render a poisonous bite.

The eagle has apparently not been observed in this area any more. On the other hand, the deer herd has increased in many parts of the state. The young deer are seen somewhat frequently in the spring of the year.

Plate 109, which is a small argillite specimen, depicts in two views a variety of fish which are found in the streams and fresh water lakes of Sussex county.

Plate No. 5 is a classic example of a simple basic multigraphic silhouette in series, which portrays the profiles of several Indians. Rapt attention to a speaker or story teller is noted in their facial expressions. The piercing eyes, thin straight mouth-lines and determined chins would indicate a certain degree of solemnity in their countenances and that possibly a serious problem is to be considered.

This argillite stone is rectangular in shape, sized 3¾"x5", and the surface is smooth. The composition demonstrates the method of converting a larger surface area to a smaller one; the physical characteristics are maintained without any apparent loss of individuality. It is also seen how the contour or structural lines are utilized.

Plate 30 in the 1960 argillite series of multigraphs is a reproduction of the entire stone with the prime details of a profile, size 2¼ inches x 2 inches. This portrait-effigy was probably an ornamental piece.

Plate 63 is a reproduction of a multigraphic composition on a medium size granitic sandstone, approximately 8 inches x 8 inches. It highlights a large individual profile, clothed apparently in a fur garment for winter weather. The head, which is directed to the left, is fully covered except for the facial features. The squinting eyes and unique nasal expression on the face would seem to point to a bitter cold or windy day. The fur design is remarkably characterized by the circular engraving.

The interesting, intricate details of Plate 119, which is an argillite specimen, size 6 inches x 4½ inches, depicts the ultimate in Indian portraiture in the 1960 series. The weather-beaten masculine facial features, with the remarkable piercing eye, aquiline nose, forceful mouth and determined chin is only matched with the strength and grandeur of his carriage. The feathered bonnet extends regally from the top of his head to beyond the neck and shoulders. The frontispiece is appropriately decorated over his well-proportioned, military-drawn chest. The erect posture expresses a degree of authority, self confidence and a ruler of men.

The New Jersey Indians were nomadic and those in the southern part of the state practiced a little agriculture. Along the eastern seaboard the evidence of deeper cavities and longer pestles would indicate the grinding of corn to a larger extent than the shallow mortars and shorter pestles to the extreme north.

The argillite specimen X-1 was found in Readington Township, which is located in the Raritan valley, in 1940. This is about eighty miles from the site in Sussex county. At the time it remained unclassified. A comparison of X-1 and X-2 which was discovered in the Sussex county site in 1960 reveals a similarity in the general characteristics and precision in the artistic workmanship. The argillite stone compares favorably with the nature of the physical qualities of those to the north.

X-1 is primarily a multigraphic composition. The principal profile depicts an Indian adorned with a feathered headpiece, indicated by the upward sweep of the lines followed by feathers down left shoulder. A band or part of the bonnet covers the head to almost the level of the eyes. The long braided hair is clearly outlined, hiding the ear area dropping downward and in front of the left shoulder and chest to a conspicuous ponytail effect.

The similarity in the eyes is remarkable. The eyes are each directed to the left. They both appear to denote a more accurate description of the anatomical counterparts of the pupils and eyelids. The profiles in each portray relatively similar forehead, aquiline nose, smooth rounded lips, mouth and chin. X-1, however, wears no attire, whereas X-2 apparently is robed in a winter garment of possibly fur pieces.

X-2 is a prime portrait, size 5"x4", on a granitic stone, the first specimen found at a site in Sussex county. The reproduction is a faithful copy of the age old engraving on stone made by an Indian of the area, which provides an accurate description of some of the physical characteristics of the native inhabitant.

With the possession of both X-1 and X-2, other specimens were studied in a painstakingly deliberate, tedious, scientific manner. From individual profiles and silhouettes it was observed that there existed a multiplicity of designs and a peculiar enmeshed conglomeration of circular and straight lines on many of the stones. The term, multigraph, was a good description of the numerous profiles, silhouettes and portraits in a given engraved composition.

X-2 portrait would appear to indicate by the elaborate robe and decorative headdress the stern countenance, powerful, broad shoulders an individual of large stature with robust health and the sovereign of his estate, a great chieftain with much power.

X-1 is a flat argillite specimen which may have been worn as a hair ornament by the feminine sex, whereas X-2 is an oval granitic, stone specimen.

Some of the highlights in the 1960 early series of the art on stone by the New Jersey Indian have recently been explored with the use of tempera.

In plates 56 and 68 there is an apparent similarity in oriental facial features, especially in the portrayal of the eyes of the silhouettes centrally located. The nose would appear to be short and aquiline. The profiles along the right borders do not resemble them. Plate 68 has a large spherical eye and plate 56 has one with a little different description of eyes than the ones situated in the internal silhouette. Both grayish brown, flat sandstones are grossly ovoid and irregular, No. 56 measures 10"x6½" and No. 68 is a little larger with 12"x7½".

The large silhouette in No. 56 occupies the major part of the left side of the stone. A wide band crosses the forehead, on top of which is the head piece. The rounded facial features and the robust and gaily garment-covered chest is directed to the left.

Both peripheral borders have profiles, the details of which can be observed on clockwise rotation.

It may be probable that the profile on the extreme peripheral right is to be noted with greater significance than the internal oriental silhouette. From a gross general view, it can be seen that the major multigraph centers on the large head, which appears to be covered with a special head dress, which extends upward from a thick band over the forehead. Below the band is the truly spherical eye, followed downward with the nose, mouth, chin and neck. The oriental silhouette now is observed to perform the function from above downward to the neck and chest line of the hair braid or a decorative fur piece.

Superimposed profiles in plate No. 75 in a peculiarly distinctive manner demonstrate the positions of individuals probably assumed while in motion. In a general view a huge figure whose profile is directed to the right would appear to be bending forward in a walking type of gait.

In the middle horizontal plane and divided by a perpendicular plane are two dissimilar profiles, one with a small spherical eye, high forehead, aquiline nose and determined mouth and chin which is facing the right. The details of the headdress extend upward along the collar line of the massive figure and to the left border in the rear. To the left of this perpendicular plane one observes several lesser profiles, directed to the left, and one with a sharper outline. The headpiece of this one extends upward on the left border to the top of the same collar band as the top of the band on the right profile.

The further observation is made in which a common hair design appears situated to the rear of both profiles, although the covering on the neck to the right is not the same as that on the left. Both of these profiles in the basal plane are in a similar upright position.

The distinctive eye markings in plate No. 47 are only matched by the clear, concise, sharp profile with symbols and designs. The ovoid sandstone specimen which is flat measures 9"x6". The facial features are directed to the left. This composition is suggestive of an historically earlier period.

In the same era, the composition on plate 50 is placed. Plate 86 is also placed in this category. No. 50 measures 7"x8" and No. 86 is a 9"x8" composition. Both profiles are directed to the left, multigraphic and literally covered with numerous symbols.

From the multigraphic maze of profiles and symbolistic designs in plate No. 85, which measures 11"x8", an interesting clue is obtained in the manner of both youthful and elderly emotional expression by rubbing noses between the male and female companions or partners. The area focused is in the left upper-horizontal plane.

In view (VA) a youthful couple would appear to be in a blissful phase of emotional expression by rubbing noses. The male, gaily decorated in his "Sunday Best," is on the right and faces the left, whereas the female spouse who is situated on the left, faces the right. The appropriately dressed female is noted to have a smooth, rounded facial contour and especially depicted is the fact that the hair appears neatly combed downward and is carried over the back of her costume. The male is remarkable for the headdress and for the resplendent finery of his clothes. This circular area is 6" in diameter.

In a reverse view of the plate (VB), a reversal of character is demonstrated. A comparison is made with (VA). The two profiles now appear older in years, and seem less enthusiastic in rubbing noses. There appears to be the indication of the accumulation of more of the worldly goods. The female member who occupies the position on the right now is facing the left. Her hairdo is changed to an upward sweep in a different style. The male partner, who is also older, occupies the left position and faces the right with an entirely new change of headdress and garment. The designs are elaborately symbolistic and appear over chest and bust.

Plate 81 is a rectangular-shaped stone specimen which measures 7½"x5½". An Indian couple appears to be strolling in a leisurely fashion along the trail. The proud, gaily decorated male, with flowing headdress and buckskin garment, is pictured in the immediate foreground with his hands and arms behind his back. The slightly smaller, more heavily set, female is situated to the right, on her partner's left, similarly attired.

A crude, three-dimensional plane composition is illustrated in plate No. 67. This composition depicts the same individual in three views. A profile of the right side of the face, a partial or two-thirds view and a full, front face view, as one can surmise by the position of the eyes, nose and mouth.

A flat ovoid sandstone specimen in plate No. 1 has a composition which measures 8¼"x6". Two elaborately dressed individuals are depicted in series, each facing the right. The larger profile on the right border, with a smile on his face, would indicate by the huge headdress and the significant ornamental decorations, one of the stature of a chieftain. The headdresses in both are noteworthy for the feathered splendor.

A classic example of a clockwise rotating multigraph is observed in plate No. 82. It is roughly triangular in shape and measures approximately 7"x7" through the perpendicular and horizontal centers, but across the tip of each rotating apex the measurement is 3½" and further down it enlarges to 4". The base for each is 7". Numerous symbolistic designs are present throughout.

Plate No. 77 is a three-dimensional multigraph. Three profiles in series. The profiles have faces directed to the extreme right, one to the left in partial sideview and the larger profile directed to the left in sharp lateral view. The decorative headdresses are similarly placed and the lower neck and chest areas would seem to be in a sort of semicircular position. The measurements are 9½"x9". The artistic quality is further enhanced by the application of bold straight line and some of the circular strokes in its basic architecture.

Plate No. 12 is an illustration of the possibilities for the application of color between the architectural design, and the latitude provided so that a clearer understanding is obtained in the portrayal, such as this Culver Lake Indian.

Among the fascinating profiles in plate No. 79, which

is visualized by the use of tempera, is that of a symbolistic, covered individual whose headdress and facial contour is directed to the left in a right side view. The neck does not appear to be clothed, but the elevated right shoulder, arm and front of the chest, together with the slightly lowered left shoulder which is similarly covered with the symbolism, may perhaps have some garment protection. Behind the right shoulder and headdress over the back there is a suggestive mass of arrows with the feathered ends protruding from a carrying case.

Plate No. 83, measuring 11"x8½", is a multigraphic composition with various profiles, but there is a silhouette in the left foreground of an individual who would appear to be in a sitting position and whose back part of the neck, right and left shoulders, arms, back and buttock, as well as the headdress and the facial features which are directed to the right, compose approximately two-thirds of the left side of the illustration.

Plate 62 is an ovoid sandstone which measures 11"x8½" for the multigraphic composition. It is noted for the many profiles, so situated in various dimensional poses, that its purpose would be to depict the important gaily decorated and singularly marked, perhaps tribal, chieftains of groups both far and near at a ceremony during which crucial decisions were considered. The headdresses are distinctly remarkable.

A massive multigraphic composition size 11"x8½" on plate 66 is noteworthy for its extravagant symbolism, especially that of a spherical marking which is ½" in diameter, situated in the upper right hand corner.

Plate No. 71 is a "rotating" multigraphic composition, rectangular in shape, and measures 7½ inches x 6½ inches.

Profiles are observed along its periphery when rotated in a clockwise manner.

Plate 4A is a multigraphic composition, size 7 inches x 4⅞" whose profiles, which are facing the right, count up to approximately ten individuals. They appear to have a common headdress, the rear of which is situated on the extreme left. The dominant figure apparently is sharply outlined on the right lower border. The reverse is plate 4B, in which a conspicuous silhouette is observed in the lower left-hand corner.

In many of the smaller argillite series, the illustrations depict profiles and silhouettes of individuals. On Plate 32 (size 4 inches x 5 inches on a stone scraper) is observed a fur winter-garbed male with lesser profiles. Plate 148 is a rectangular argillite specimen, size 4½"x3¾", centrally situated which exhibits the architecture of the headdress, face, neck and upper part of the body. Plate 91 is a smaller effigy-like specimen in argillite of a male individual. Plate 30 is another argillite of the same portrait-like significance. This is remarkable in its architectural design in showing the details of the eyes, face and the feathers.

Some of the intricate details can be seen in plates 10 and 11 demonstrating the engraving effect with the application of the "circular-straight line" technique. The basic architectural design without the use of color is produced. Masterful multigraphic compositions of profiles and silhouettes are endowed with artistic subtlety.

Plate 11 is a description of a male. The spherical eye, nose, mouth and chin are followed by a well-proportioned neck, with part of the hair falling gently over the right shoulder and chest. The entire head is attired in an elaborate headdress. The long hair appears braided or tied at the level of the neck and shoulder. The facial markings are directed to the right. If the plate is reversed from A to B or rotated clockwise to an upside-down view, there is a change in the total architecural display and a complete change of characterization.

The features are altered with the profile in the left position. The forehead appears to contain a supporting band to the headdress. Below the forehead is the spherical eye, but apparently it is now situated above the left eyebrow. The nose is somewhat stubby, but the mouth, lips and chin are prominent. The left ear level area has a tied hair braid or some ornamental material which hides the ear itself and drops downward over the left shoulder.

Plate 10 is a multigraphic composition. A very prominent spherical eye is noted in the large profile. Vestiges of head feathers rise on top of the headpiece. The neck and shoulder are rather thick and heavy. A series of partial silhouettes are situated to the right of the major composition. Reversal of this plate illustrates the principle observed in plate 11.

AMERICAN INDIAN OF NEW JERSEY

PLATES

1960 SERIES

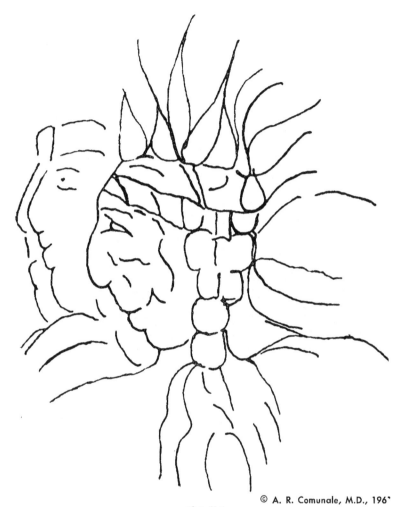

Plate X-1
— Raritan —
Reddington (Somerville)
Portrait
Actual Size—1940
80 Miles from Sussex County, N. J.
Chalky Argillite (white)

Plate X-2
— 1st Specimen —
Gramitic, Exact Reproduction
Sussex County, 1960

Plate 21
. Head, Face and Neck
Side View—Argillite
Sussex County, 1960

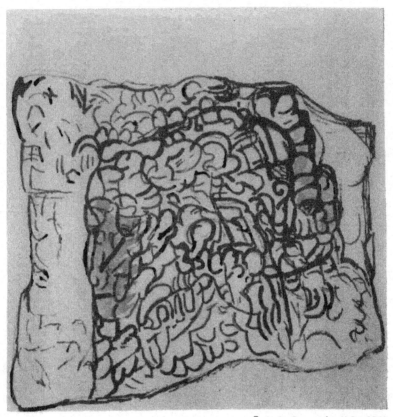

Plate 23
Head and Face
⅔ View on Argillite Stone
Actual Size
Sussex County, 1960

Plate 59
Argillite, Left Side of Head,
Face, and Neck, Actual Size
Sussex County, 1960

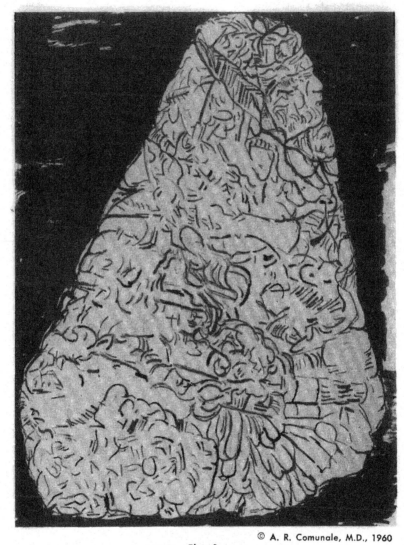

Plate 0
Young Squaw With Robe
Sussex County, 1960

Plate 142
Granite Sandstone
Specimen with effigy characteristics,
and numerous multigraphic signs, symbols,
profiles.

Plate 58
Silhouette, Heads and Right Side Arm
Actual Size
Sussex County, 1960

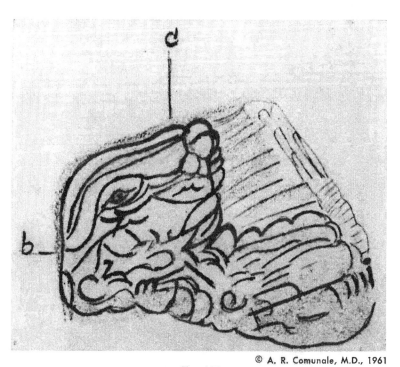

Plate 112
B—Deer Fawn Head, Vertical
C—Argillite, Rattlesnake Head, Horizontal
Sussex County, 1960

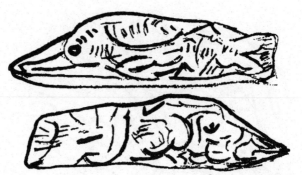

Plate 109
Argillite, Fish
Actual Size, Two Views
Sussex County, 1960

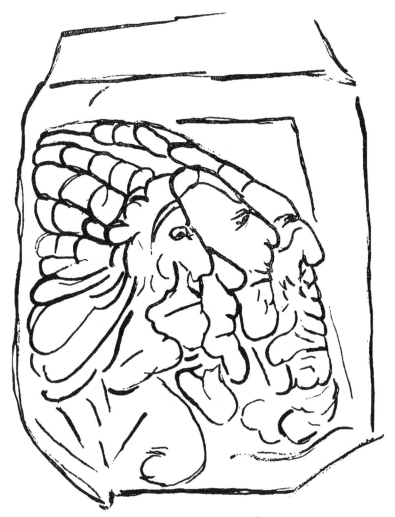

© A. R. Comunale, M.D., 1961

Plate 5
Multigraphic Silhouette
Argillite, Actual Size
Sussex County, 1960

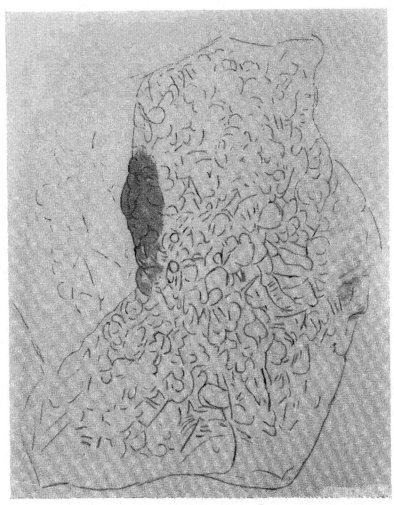

Plate 63
Multigraphic Composition
Granite Sandstone
Profile in Winter Garments
Sussex County, 1960

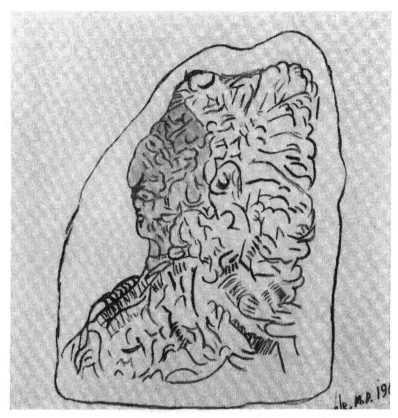

© A. R. Comunale, M.D., 1961

Plate 119
Portrait—Head, Chest
Actual Size, Argillite
Sussex County, 1960

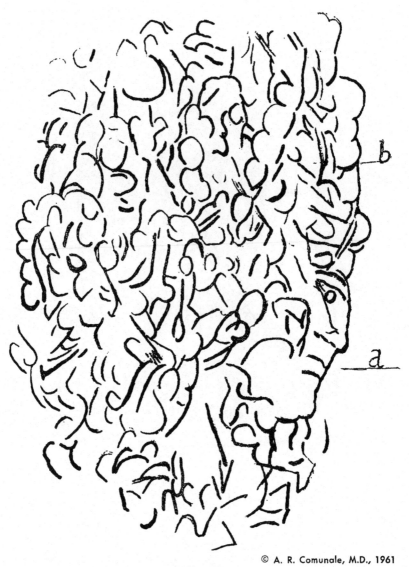

Plate 11
Reversibility of Character
Actual Size, Portraits (a), (b)
Sussex County, 1960

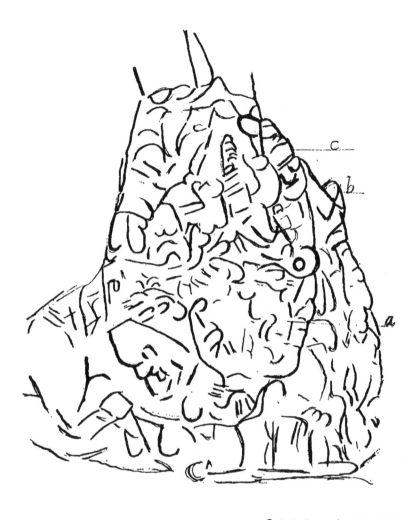

Plate 10
Composition with Reversibility of Character, a, b, c
Actual Size
Sussex County, 1960

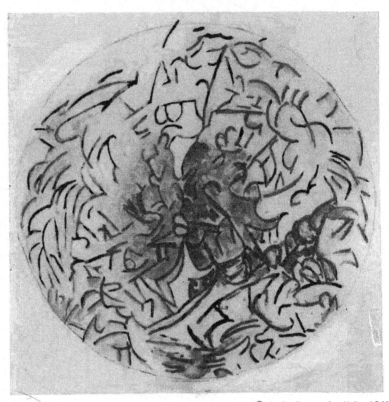

Plate 85
Multigraph on Stone, 6x6
Two Profiles Rubbing Noses
Sussex County, 1960

DESCRIPTION
OF
1961 SERIES

In 1961 a collection of over thirty stone specimens were obtained, which on careful examination and study exhibited multigraphic compositions attributed to Indian artists of many years ago. An analysis of some of the details was attempted by the use of the transferral of their exact reproduction from the stone, where possible, to construction paper and also as an extra aid, the application of water color which in many cases animated the specific architectural design and subject matter intended for portrayal by the Indian author of the period.

Each multigraph was measured and the size was recorded in inches. Thirty-two plates were completed to date in this series. The plates are now described individually.

Plate 1, a multigraphic composition on stone, size 8″x 9½″ depicts a portrait in the upright position, facing the left. Satisfaction and contentment are noted in the facial expression. The neck is encircled by a ruffled-type garment. The left shoulder is prominently displayed. The large headdress drops smoothly down the neck, shoulder and upper part of the back.

On complete rotation of the plate a secondary, elaborate profile can be observed, with a lesser one above it.

Section R—plate 1 illustrates a circular type engraving of the face, neck and hair outline. The rounded contour and the hairdo would appear to denote a member of the feminine sex.

Section B is a winter-garbed profile of the right side

49

of the head and neck which is located at the base of the upright portrait.

Lesser figures are situated internally.

Plate 2—A multigraph, size 6″x3¾″ on stone, has a profile which is directed to the left of a prominent feminine individual. The forehead, nose, lips and chin characteristics are typically feminine. The forehead is high and rounded, nose rounded, lips not exaggerated and the chin is small and rounded. The neck and chest are covered with a hair braid which flows downward across the left shoulder to the bustline. There is an apparent absence of feathers.

Several profiles are directed to the right and comprise the back, which gives the appearance of a pouch like garment.

When the plate is reversed, an older feminine individual is noted which is directed to the right. The headdress has a shawl-like effect. The profiles that are directed to the left comprise the rear view of the hair braids. The contour of the forehead, nose and narrow receding lips would suggest the loss of teeth. The rounded chin and neckline are not remarkable, except for the descriptive garment over the chest which faces the right.

Plate 3—a multigraph on stone, size 7¾″x7¾″, has a prominent portrait facing the left. Three others are also included in this view.

3—B depicts a very decorative hairdo, which extends down over the left shoulder. No feathers are noted. The contour of the head, nose, chin and neckline would indicate an individual of the feminine sex. The hairdo appears to be tied at the level of the shoulder.

Section 3—C is observed when plate 3 is reversed.

Plate 4 depicts a portrait on stone, size 8″x7″. The left

features are visualized with typical linear and circular engraving. The nose appears long and straight with a portion of the forehead exposed from under the headpiece. The lips are not exaggerated. The chin is tilted and the neck and chest line follow the chin gracefully. The long sweeping lines at the base complete the contour of the composition.

Two lesser silhouettes at 45 degrees, clockwise, form an arc of a semicircle along the circumference facing the right. Full rotation to 90 degrees reveals a full silhouette. The lines which form the base of the previous silhouette now depict a series of minor ones and face the right. A large over-all silhouette is directed to the left.

Plate 5—A multigraph on stone, size 5"x9½", depicts a striking profile which is directed to the right. Another profile makes up the winter headdress. In reverse position a lesser profile is noted. When the plate is reversed, the multigraph on this copper-colored stone exhibits a profile directed to the right which has a spherical eye design, small nose, unexaggerated lips and a round chin. The profiles on the left are now distinctly different. The one which previously occupied the base is now observed as a large silhouette at the top, followed downward by the features of a lesser profile, and the chest being the framework of an inverted profile.

Plate 6—A, multigraphic composition on stone, size 5"x2¾", has a prominent profile directed to the left. The descriptive forehead, nose, mouth and chin appear to be masculine. Some strands of loose hair stray over the forehead. Directed to the right are several profiles; one is located above the hairline to the rear and the other completes the back of the neck area. The thick hair braid across

51

both the right and left features falls down the shoulder areas of a winter garb, including the symbolistic and tribal markings.

In reverse, there are three profiles facing the left and four which face the right.

Plate 7—a multigraphic composition on stone size 6"x5" is centrally located. This depicts a female tribal member. The contour of the facial features, head and neck is rounded. Profusely flowing hair sweeps over the neck, left shoulder and bustline. Closer inspection reveals a series of lesser profiles directed to the left from above downward. Along the periphery several others are directed to the right which become a part of the hair framework. Symbolistic designs are noted over the face and the major portion of the composition.

Plate 8—A, multigraph on stone, size 4¾"x6", has five profiles directed to the right in series. (8-A-B-C-D-E). Profiles A and D consist of three features from above downward, with a common hairdress, neck and chest garment. Profiles C-D-E are individuals with a common feathered headdress. The contour lines descriptively illustrate each.

Directed to the left are four profiles, in which the feathers compose the architecture of the nose, mouth and chin. Emphasis is placed on the silhouette directed to the right.

Plate 9—A, multigraphic composition on stone, size 6½" x8½", reveals a portrait, depicting the left side of the head, face and neck. Details of the head-piece extend over the left shoulder. Symbolistic designs appear over the features of the face. Secondary silhouettes are directed to the left. Another begins with the lines of the upper lips and bottom of the chin upward.

On either side are two others. The larger secondary one extends downward from the level of the ear to below the neck line.

Directed to the right in an opposite view along the periphery are five lesser silhouettes cascading from the top of the headdress to the left shoulder below.

Plate 10—a profile on stone, size 5"x6", aided by color and forces of light, exhibits an individual clothed in a garment which extends down and over the left shoulder and back. Determination is expressed in the facial features, aquiline nose, thin mouth, medium-sized forehead and prominent chin. The eyes appear round and the neck shows no evidence of goiter or disease of the thyroid gland. The head piece denotes the characteristic decoration of a male person.

Plate 11—a multigraphic profile on stone, size 6"x9½". In position A it elicits a composition with features directed to the right. The headdress of feathers is apparently high, with the hair falling over the right shoulder. The side view of the face reveals a high forehead, descriptive eyes, aquiline nose, thin mouth but a prominent chin.

Plate 11B depicts the details of the contour lines of the forehead, nose, mouth and chin. Watercolor is selected for the purpose of illustration.

Plate 12—a multigraph on stone, size 6"x10", is especially profuse with symbolistic designs, which are situated between the various division planes that form the borders of the profiles. A large profile is located facing the right and is represented by a neatly tied hair lock. The hair covers the neck and shoulder. No attempt is made with this view or the one in reverse for the application of color, so that the display of the symbols and signs may be brought into focus. In the reverse plate there are five profiles, three directed to the left and two to the right. The straight lines are sharp.

Plate 13—a multigraph on stone, size 8"x9½", has two profiles in the upright position, one on the right and one on the left, which appear to be clothed in winter garments. A stone ornament is observed on the hair braid at the level of the right ear.

Two features are observed when the plate is rotated clockwise at 45 degrees, in the right lower position, and two others on full 90 degrees rotation, in the right and left position.

About the periphery of the multigraph there are six distinct profiles, and one centrally in the upright position appears to face the other as a couplet.

Plate 14—a multigraph on stone, size 6"x8", is unique in its composition. In the upright position several profiles are each directed to the left and several to the right. A common bond appears to exist in the hair braids, like the union of "Siamese twins," which falls entwined down the neck, back and shoulder of each profile. An expression of authority is observed in the right one, whereas on the left it is that of a "command."

Projection 14 on the left depicts the details of the tribal markings on the face, head adornment and/or ornaments about the neck. Projection 14 on the right and secondary profiles appear in the composition. In 14 A-R and 14 B-L projections, the elaborate hairdos and headpieces portray the distinctive native style of the period.

Plate 15—a multigraph on stone, size 9"x6½", illustrates the reversibility of character in the features of silhouettes, portraits and profiles by simple rotation, usually in a clockwise manner.

In the upright position a profile which is directed to the left shows a youthful feminine figure with a large band across the forehead that controls the hairdo. The contour of the face appears rounded and graceful. A profile directed to the right appears to jut out from the hairdo in the rear, at the bottom of which are the features of a lesser profile. This comprises the lower part of the hair outline.

By gentle clockwise rotation, in a secondary plane, five to six profiles are observed directed to the right. Profile 15-R with its details is observed at 45 degrees rotation, and in a 90 degrees rotation profiles are observed in other planes facing the right. Details are noted in plate 15-A-R with reproductions of the symbolism and tribal markings.

Plate 16—a profile on stone, size 4½"x5½", depicts the details of the right side of the face. A band appears to encircle the hair from the back and across the forehead. The braid of hair on the right seems to fall in front of the chest and over the shoulder. A member of importance in the tribe is indicated by the determined chin, thin mouth and the descriptive eyes and nose.

Plate 17—a multigraph on stone, size 5"x6", depicts a profile which is located in the central upright position. Four profiles are observed by clockwise rotation at 90 degrees along the periphery to the right and several facing the left. Profiles are also seen in the reverse view located both on the right and on the left.

Plate 18—a "tracing-drawing," with the significant circular-straight line effect containing symbolistic designs, illustrates some of the qualities of the basic architecture in a composition of an Indian portrait.

The feathers, which are prominently displayed in the headdress, down to the intricate details of the material covering the front of the chest and the anatomy of the face, produce a unique, unmatched effect, not described anywhere. Tribal markings and symbols are noted.

Plate 19—a multigraph on stone, size 6"x7¾", exhibits the profiles in a peripheral position on the right and also on the left. In the central area, silhouettes on the right and left are reversed and face each other. One large profile, on the lower two-thirds of the right, faces the left and depicts the features of an individual, including the head, neck, shoulders and chest. The hair covers the left shoulder.

Plate 20—a multigraphic silhouette on stone, size 10"x 5½", is characterized by circular engraving. Both a right and a left profile are observed in the upright position. Two separately distinct features are seen in the reverse view.

Plate 21—a profile on stone, size 5¼"x3¾" facing the right, has a preponderance of circular engraving. The features show contentment. A healthy young female is revealed in the hairdo, forehead, aquiline nose, thin lips, prominent chin and good neck line.

Plate 22—a multigraphic composition on stone, size 6"x3¾", has a prominent silhouette facing the right with a high headpiece. The neck is covered. The forehead is arched and the nose is aquiline. The hair braid comes over the right shoulder. Tribal markings are noted on the face. Directed to the left are three lesser profiles.

In reverse or full rotation, full features of a profile are observed on the left and also one along the periphery on the right. Lesser figures are directed to the right.

Plate 23—a silhouette on stone, size 5¼"x5", which with the application of color and the directed display of light reveal the basic architecture and the purpose of the original author to portray an individual of that era.

Plate 24—a multigraph on stone, size 4½"x5", depicts

the principal profile, which is directed to the right. A lesser internal profile is directed to the left, which forms part of the rear view of the hair braid. The headdress is of a winter design. The contour of the forehead, nose, mouth, chin and thick neck with its heavy, fatty folds denotes the profile of a heavy-set individual. Slight clockwise rotation and the neck folds form another profile below the first. A large silhouette is observed on complete rotation which is directed to the right.

Plate 25—a profile on stone, size 6″x10″, depicts a member of the tribe with a distinctive head piece. The covering over the neck, shoulders, back and torso is indicative of winter attire. The stern expressive determined features probably denote a male member. The forehead appears a little higher, the eye is spherical, the nose aquiline and the lips are thin. The folds of skin down the neck line would indicate a heavy-set older individual.

Plate 26—a multigraph on stone, size 6¾″x7″, illustrates a composition with a combination of multiple faces, subtly divided by planes, and the manner in which large surface areas, such as the extent involved by each individual profile, become fully integrated into a mathematically smaller homogenous mass of profiles into a smaller area.

Faces are observed on the right, left and in reverse. Each profile appears to have a special descriptive design for the anatomy of the eye in either the upright or retroverted position. Singular detail is also noted in the details of the nose, mouth, chin and headdress. Facial markings are exhibited in special projections for each individual.

The adaptation of color to each pattern has an animating effect. The bare profiles are thus visualized in their proper perspective.

Plate 26X—illustrates the utilization of the essential

structural elements in the phase of reduction from a larger surface area to a smaller one.

Plate 26Y—illustrates the individual structural components of each profile, released from the multigraphic maze. Plate 26-A is another example.

Plate 27—a multigraph on stone, size 4½"x9½", is a composition which has a large silhouette, with its face directed to the right. The torso, buttocks and hips are depicted in a side view. The long hair extends in braids on both the right and left, then downward over the back. These braids are subtly utilized in a unique composition of cascading profiles which are illustrated in alternate positions. One set is observed in the upright position and the other in reverse, on the left. The right braid has one face directed to the right, two to the left and several in reverse.

The anterior part of the torso is covered by robe.

Plate 27—A illustrates by the use of color the composition of the four profiles which are directed to the right along the periphery of the multigraph. Arrows denote the planes' division. 27—B is a detailed illustration of the lower portion of the upright position of plate 27. There are three profiles which face the left. They are colored for illustrative purposes to clarify the basic architectural design. This composition has an area of three full profiles, but in a reduced phase.

27—C illustrates the extent of an area to which the profiles were reduced, in the rear of the torso, making up what appears to consist of braided hair down the back.

There are identification marks in the anatomy of each dissected profile from the multigraph, specifically denoting the location or relative position in the architectural design.

Two profiles facing the right have a feather in common. One is situated at the level of the ear line and the other

58

can be seen in a braid below the neck line. The profile facing the left has a feather located on the top of the head.

The two profiles in a left sided view have what appears to be two large inverted U's and two double lines. In one they are located in the collar area of the garment, and in the other profile they can be seen on the middle upper portion of the hair.

The significance of these marks has not been determined further, but the position of the identification marks in relation to the anatomy illustrate how a given surface area is utilized in the reduction of a combined area without loss of its essential structural elements.

Each profile has distinctive and descriptive contour lines of the eyes, nose, mouth and chin, including the tribal markings and symbolism.

Plate 28—a multigraph on stone, size 9¾"x6¾", has a profile in the upright position, with an artistic quality to the contour lines. Two profiles are facing to the right. In the reverse plate multiple profiles are directed to the left.

This composition has many circular and straight lines.

Plate 29—a multigraph on stone, size 5"x8½", depicts an interesting profile with a large headdress that is directed to the left in a two-thirds view. On the extreme left, feathers from the headdress are observed, which complete the profile of a lesser figure and perhaps the feathered ends of arrow shafts protruding from their carrying case.

Lesser profiles are directed to the right, which form a robe or garment that appears as being carried over the shoulder.

When the plate is reversed, distinct multiple profiles are observed which are directed both to the left and some to the right.

Plate 30—a multigraphic silhouette on stone, size

6½"x9¾", displays a very high headdress, its profile directed to the right. A small portion of the forehead is exposed. The eyes are descriptive, the nose aquiline, long mouth-line with narrow lips and jutting chin. The neck appears to be covered with a smooth-fitting attire which resembles a collar. Symbolistic circular engraving is present throughout.

Plate 31—a multigraph on stone, size 6"x9¾", depicts a distinguished main profile in the upright position which is directed to the left.

31—A . . . this profile illustrates the basic architecture involving the circular and straight line engraving. 31—B . . . this profile with color detail is directed to the left. 31—C, a reversed plate, reveals a multigraphic silhouette with detail. The prominent profile is now directed to the right. 31—D, in reverse, depicts many profiles directed to the right. 31—E is a profile situated in the lower part of the multigraph in the reverse position.

Plate 32—a multigraph on stone, size 8"x8¾", has a series of six profiles, which are illustrated separately. They are situated both centrally and along the periphery. As a whole, the multigraphic composition appears rounded. The main theme occupies about two-thirds of the area and the lesser ones comprise the left outer border.

32—B . . . is the profile of an important member of the tribe or chieftain. The head is lowered and the large feathers fall gently to the rear. A fluffy design surrounding the neck is visible and covers the broad chest, and resembles a winter garment or cloak.

32—B . . . begins to the rear of the hair line of 32—A. The features appear sharp and solemn, with flowing head feathers. In both plates the long artistic free-flowing base lines can be noted, which form the coiled hair or braid cascading down the back of the robe.

32—AA—a young masculine profile; front of the robe's neck seems to be designed for keeping it open in a loose manner or tightening the garment. It is situated anterior to 32—A.

Along the periphery facing the left are two profiles 32—AL and 32—BL. Plate 32—R at 45 degrees depicts an elaborately dressed masculine figure with unique features and a gaily displayed turban-like headdress much similar to an Arabian sheik.

PLATES

1961 SERIES

Multigraphs
Profiles
Portraits
Silhouettes

Plate 1
8x9½ Portrait on Stone
Sussex County, 1962

Plate 2
Multigraphic Silhouette on Stone
6x3¾—Sussex County, 1961

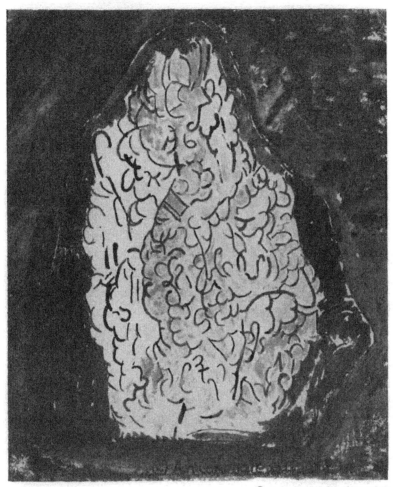

Plate 7
Argillite Stone 6x5
Silhouette
Sussex County

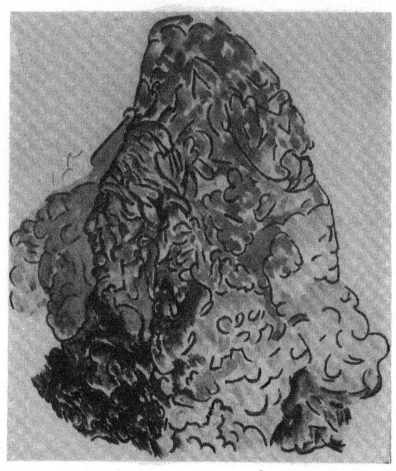

Plate 9
Portrait on Stone, 6½x8½
Sussex County, 1961

Plate 12
6"x10"
Profiles on Stone
Sussex County, 1961

Plate 13
8″x9½″ Multigraph on Stone
Sussex County, 1961

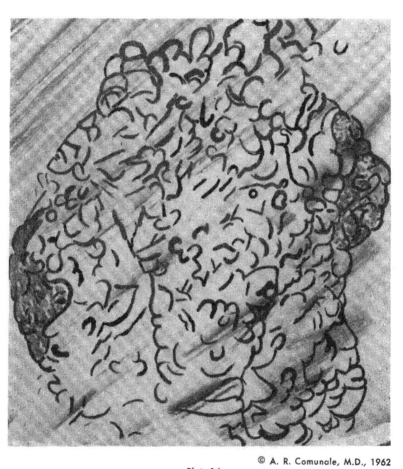

Plate 14
6"x8" Multigraph on Stone
Profiles
Sussex County

© A. R. Comunale, M.D., 1962

Plate 18
6"x8" Portrait on Stone
Sussex County, 1962

Plate 27-C
Profiles from Multigraph on Stone
Sussex County

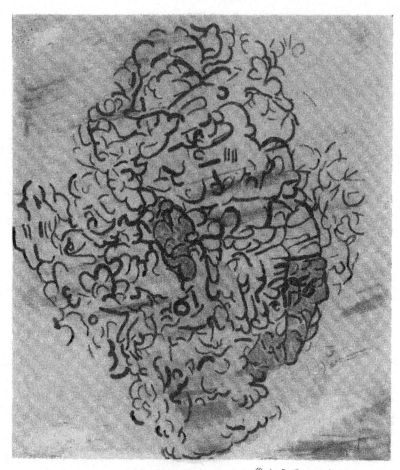

Plate 28
9¾ x 6¾
Profiles on Stone
Sussex County

Plate 32
8x8¼ Multigraph on Stone
Sussex County

EFFIGIES

Effigies are usually rather peculiar characters and specimens occurring in various sizes and shapes, as well as on different kinds of stone. The sandstone variety are more numerous.

Plate 37 is a granitic sandstone specimen, size 4½"x3". Its reproduction is that of the entire stone. The surface is uniquely illustrated with the contour lines. The periphery is smooth, rounded with a sanded effect. Rotating the specimen will produce changes in the character of profiles.

Plate 31 is an argillite stone specimen depicting by contour lines a multigraphic effigy-like profile. It is 4 inches x 2 inches. The features are sharply carved. The stone is triangular with a smooth rounded apex.

Plate No. 18 is an argillite effigy-like stone. It is 4½"x3" in size. In the H position, illustrated, the profiles on the right border are noted with a maze of multigraphic compositions internally. In the R position, one may be surprised to see the effigy-like figure of a bear, with its snout directed to the left. As usual, if the entire plate is reversed one cannot fail to see the profiles in series which are directed to the right.

Plate No. 78 has similar aspects as that observed in plate 142.

An interesting triangular sandstone effigy is observed in plate 73 which measures 7"x3". The apex is pointed and at the base profiles and silhouettes are seen, directed to either side and in the middle. If held by the apex, all the profiles are viewed with their faces directed to the right.

Not all stone effigies are descriptive of individuals alone. It is not unusual to find various sizes of specimens depicted in a gross fashion. Plate No. 72 measures 8 inches by 5 inches and illustrates an unclassified animal like a rabbit in the sitting position. The entire surface is also profusely covered with symbols and undifferentiated profiles.

Larger effigies not suitable for tracing were photographed. The transparencies indicate on film the nature of the specimens as they appear in a general sense.

"Carvings" are usually noted in the argillite collection. The sculptured work indicate the features of Indians in profile and appear to be ornamental rather than for any other purpose.

New Jersey is a state which can proudly say that its aborigines at one time had a high degree of art culture, Their stone artistic memoirs unfold, for all to see, the photographic panorama of the era, life and customs.

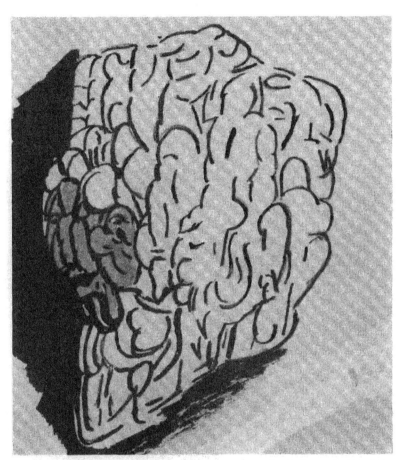

Plate 37
Portrait
Face, Head and Neck Piece
Argillite, Actual Size
Sussex County, 1960

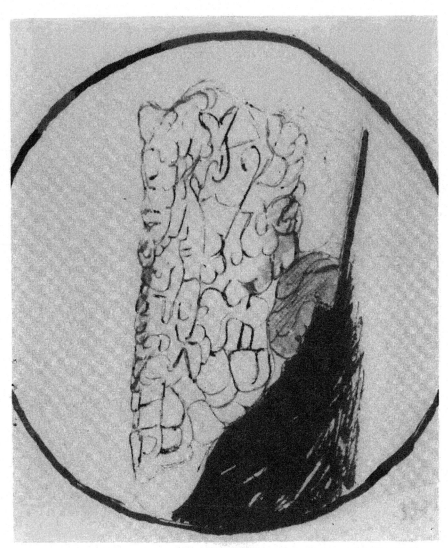

Plate 31
Silhouette
Argillite, Knife
Actual Size
Sussex County, 1960

EFFIGY

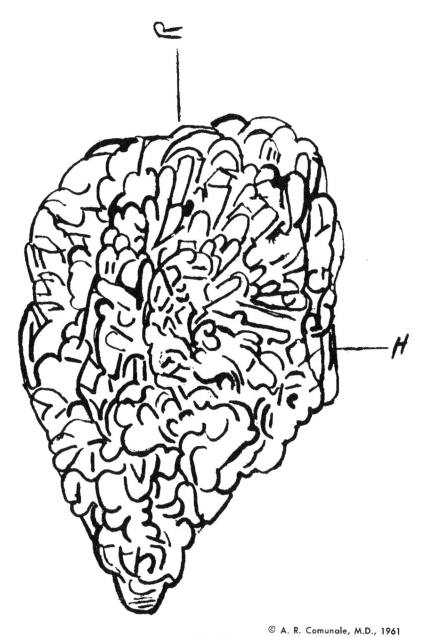

H

Plate 18
Ornamental, Multigraphic—H, Bear—R, Profiles
Argillite, Actual Size
Sussex County, 1960

Plate 30
Portrait, Chief
Argillite, Actual Size
Sussex County, 1960

PICTOGRAPHS

Prehistoric man sketched various animals on the walls of caves with an intriguing dexterity and rhythmic expression of motion. The application of color is amazing with the limited, basic, crude material at hand.

A field of unexplored Indian art of perhaps a later day on rocks is now being studied. Scenes on some of the argillite stones, classified as pictographs, ably demonstrate both motion and still-life. The illustrations depict the forces of the hunt and the existing animal life of the era, which in their eyes were considered either interesting or vital for their existence. When the white man came and destroyed the forests and plowed the fields, it was a severe blow in which the Indian was unaccustomed and difficult to reconcile.

A scene depicting the successful native hunter on his return to a cave or home may be observed in plate 60. The satisfied expression of a female companion is seen. She, standing on the side to the right, watches him joyfully as he enters, carrying a large male deer or elk, whose head and foreparts over the right shoulders are apparently being supported or held by the hindquarters with both hands in front.

This rear-view scene would indicate two purposes. First, the large deer is of prime consideration. Secondly, there is a desire to exhibit the strong masculine muscular development, especially noted in the fine muscles of the back, broad shoulders, athletic back and chest, with well-proportioned hips. The lower extremities such as the legs and feet are not visible, either because they are of lesser importance or perhaps he is only of average height.

The happy, contented, feminine individual situated on the right, with rounded contours of the face and neck, has loose strands of hair that is not combed and which strays over the face, neck and left shoulder. The argillite stone is rectangular in shape on which this pictograph is present.

Several facets of interest are seen in Plate 111. A still-life composition is visualized with a large bird sitting on a nest over the rounded eggs. The breast does not completely cover the oval eggs. The tail feathers are conspicuously long. The head and beak would indicate a species of the eagle family. In both the eagle and hawk the beak is curved long and the upper part protrudes over and beyond the lower portion.

Just anterior to the head of the nesting bird is revealed the larger facial contour of an Indian. Forming the border is the hair, forehead, eye, nose, mouth and rounded chin. The tail feathers of the bird are now substituted for the Indian's head feathers on the right of the headpiece. The correlation is that feathers which appear in his war bonnet are obtained from this great bird.

This argillite specimen measures 3 inches by 2½ inches. Clockwise rotation to about 45 degrees is the profile of an individual which is directed to the right. The significant tail feathers of the bird are now representative of the hair braid which drops perpendicularly to the neck and shoulder on the right. The egg design represents some undisclosed feature to the details of the silhouette. The thick heavy-set neck can be seen at the base and to the left of the feather-hair composition.

Further clockwise rotation reveals a profile whose fea-

Plate 60
Argillite, Pictograph
Anatomy of the Muscles of the Back
Carrying Deer

Plate 111
Bird with Eggs on Nest
and Silhouette
Argillite, Actual Size
Sussex County, 1960

PICTOGRAPH

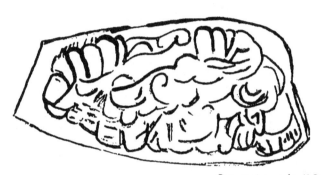

Plate 113
Argillite, Woodchuck
Actual Size
Sussex County, 1960

PICTOGRAPH

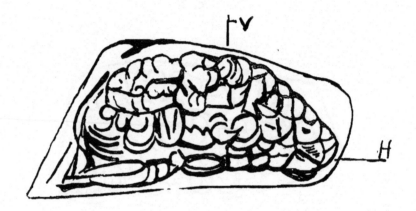

Plate 116
Argillite, Copperhead Snake—H
Actual Size, Silhouette—V
Sussex County, 1960

tures are directed to the left. The oval egg design is situated superior to and in the same horizontal plane as the bird's tail feathers.

Many indigenous animals are still present and can be observed along the roadside occasionally. They usually escape beneath the stony fencerows which divide the farm lands or serve as property lines. The common woodchuck is a furry mammal which resembles a small beaver. The tail appears flat but is bushy with long hair. The wily male runs as swiftly as a small nondescript dog. They get fat and appear subtly lazy until disturbed. Then they seek their burrows in haste, to which they escape and seek refuge.

The woodchuck is considered a vermin, although he feeds on an herbivorous diet of clover and alfalfa but, because of the numerous burrows which are a serious hazard to the dairy cows, is to be destroyed at the slightest provocation by man. The holes or outlets of these burrows are unseen traps which become hidden by the growing succulent green grass on which the dairy cattle feed and roam, only to get a foot caught and usually result in a broken leg during the fall to the ground. The cow is eventually a serious liability.

This argillite specimen is 3 inches by 1½ inches. The head of the animal is directed to the left and the well-depicted tail is observed at the base on the right. On rotation of this Plate 113, profiles are noted.

MAPS

In a series of three argillite specimens, which are neither tools, knives, scrapers nor ornaments, one observes a unique characteristic apart from the multigraphs, pictographs, effigies or carvings. Each appears to describe in the manner of a map such areas of interest or territory, direction, description and information pertinent to a given location, including the possible specific individuals involved.

Plate 14, measuring 4½"x2¾", would appear to resemble the state of New Jersey. It was found in Frankford Township of Sussex county in 1960. The border on the right resembles the Atlantic ocean and the coastline which is so prominent with its summer resorts, swimming, bathing, fishing and boating.

Two profiles are noted from above downward which subtly compose the eastern border and shoreline of the state.

On the left or western border is noted a roughening of its irregular outline, which describes the course of the Delaware river. Three individual profiles are directed to the left and their outlines comprise the western border of the state. The western border and the eastern coastline unite in a protuberance forming the southern tip of the state at Cape May and Atlantic City.

The geological stratification of the argillite specimen appears to have lines in such an appropriate manner and direction which may possibly indicate that they were utilized specifically for the geographical distribution of territory, such as for hunting purposes. The profiles which are located in the prescribed areas denote the ruling chieftains of the areas so designated.

Besides the division of the hunting grounds one may assume that some of the long lines across the state indicate various trails. One of the famous and important trails is the Minisink Trail which starts in the upper reaches of Sussex county and traverses New Jersey like a river with its accessary and subsidiary tributaries in a southeasterly direction to the coast.

Sussex county is located in the upper northwest corner of the state. The quiet peaceful countryside is a dairyland among the rolling alpine mountains with its cool, crystal-clear mountain streams in which the native trout abound. The deer herd is allowed to roam through fertile green fields of alfalfa or clover and when pressed, escape in a leisurely manner through the protective, tall, dense forest stands whose timber is conserved in a scientific forestation plan.

Plate 16 is a rectanguar argillite specimen, size 4¾"x4". The remarkable features designated are the following: an Indian chief whose profile and facial outlines are directed to the right. Situated between the area which would form the braid of hair on the side of the neck, face and scalp is an irregular outline of a lake. This irregularity begins at the base of the specimen and is seen to converge in a winding manner at the top in large semicircles.

A study of the area in which this specimen originates would indicate the body of water to be Culvers Lake. The surrounding area denotes where the Indian resides. The face is directed to the right which is located along the north-easterly shoreline, along which trails, noted by the irregular curved lines, hug the high bluff on the north side along the mountain. These trails pursue a northerly course in the

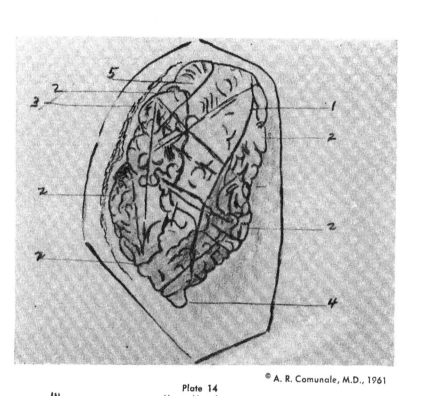

© A. R. Comunale, M.D., 1961

Plate 14
Map—New Jersey
Argillite, Actual Size
Sussex County, 1960
1. Trails
2. Chiefs
3. Delaware River
4. Coast Line
5. Sussex County

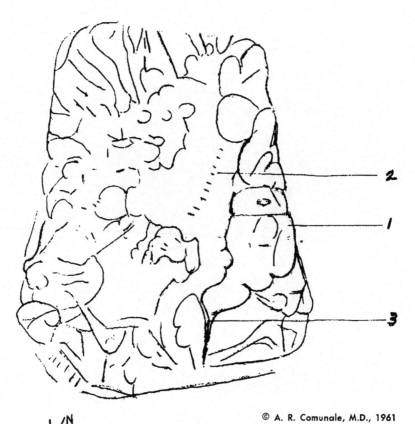

Plate 16
Map, Argillite, Actual Size
1. Indian Chief, 2. Culvers Lake
3. Trails North,
Sussex County, 1960

N
S

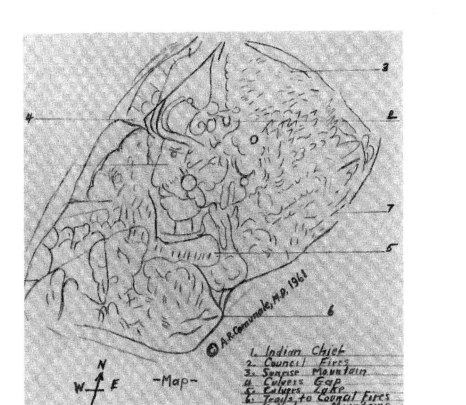

Plate 15
1. Indian Chief
2. Council Fires
3. Sunrise Mountain
4. Culvers Gap
5. Culvers Lake
6. Trails to Council Fires
7. Kittatinny Mountains
   Argillite, Actual Size
   Sussex County, 1960

direction of the Delaware River up to the council fires of the Minisink Indians.

Plate 15, whose size is 6½ inches by 4½ inches, exhibits an unusual description of an area in a unique array of symbols and signs, which also include the incorporation of a profile. This latter has the eye truly spherical beneath the contours of the eyebrow. Artistically descriptive beyond question is the profile outline of the forehead, nose, mouth-line, chin and neck. The manner of the headdress with its individual detail could only be that of an important sovereign or chieftain. A large oval decorative piece is situated on the left side of the face. Below the prominent forceful chin is the neckline which is completed by the outline of the robe-covered chest and right shoulder.

Also interspersed in this composition are the Kittatinny mountains which are situated along the northeasterly corner with the meandering trails which lead to the council fires in the north. Sunrise Mountain is located in the upper northern tip. Facing the southwestern part in an area of the face and neck is Culvers Lake and the Gap in the mountain in 4 and 5 positions.

Circular areas in 2 position are the council fires location where it is presumed the important surrounding tribes held their official meetings.

The Culvers Lake Indian has hereby given a vivid description of himself, his general appearance and location of his residence, important land marks, such as the gap in the mountains, the large body of water in Culvers Lake, trails through the mountains and the direction to the council fires.

SPECIFICATIONS

Specifications followed in preparing this book:

1. Nature of stone; type; color and surface location.

2. Size; measurements.

3. Method of determination of objective findings.

a. Direct study of specimen for subject matter.

b. Tracing of clinical material with soft lead pencil followed by India ink.

c. Direct drawing from specimen.

d. Transferral of tracing copy over carbon paper to heavy art paper; size #100 and applying India ink over reproduction.

4. Separation of objective findings and classification for illustrative purposes.

5. Description of findings:

a. Character of art; circular or cubical; straight-line or angular; mixed linear and circular; sculpture or carving and flaking.

b. Artistic arrangement and structure . . . anatomical structure of the eyes; nose; head and face in portraits and silhouettes; multiplicity; reversibility and change of character.

c. Nature of objective material . . . portraits; silhouettes; source of food supply (animals; fish; birds; turtles; deer; moose; snakes) maps; pictograms; engravings on tools; effigies both small and large (markers).

6. Description of area at the site and its relation to trails in New Jersey.

CPSIA information can be obtained at www.ICGtesting.com
Printed in the USA
BVOW06s0437300916

463764BV00032B/90/P